THE OFFICIAL ENGLAND RUGBY ANNUAL 2012

Written by Martin Johnston
Designed by Jane Greig

ENGLAND RUGBY

© 2011. Published by Grange Communications Ltd., Edinburgh under licence from the RFU. The England Rose is an official trade mark of the Rugby Football Union and is the subject of extensive trade mark registration worldwide. Printed in the EU.

Photography © RFU and Action Images

ISBN: 978-1-908221-23-0

£7.99

Contents

All information and statistics were correct at the end of the 2010-11 RBS 6 Nations and before the 2011 Rugby World Cup.

Introduction

Welcome to the Official England Rugby Annual for 2012. As usual there are in-depth articles, fun features and great pictures of all your favourite players.

This year we look at the team behind the England team and at some of the clubs where the senior players started their careers. We also reveal a few things you probably didn't know about Twickenham, the home of England Rugby.

There's the usual round-up on the RBS 6 Nations and as ever, we check in with the England Saxons, Sevens and Under 20s squads. We also look at the best young players with the ever popular 'Four to Watch' feature and put the spotlight on key members of the senior squad.

There's plenty of fun to be had too with The Big England Quiz, a player-inspired game of Top Trumps and other tricky puzzles.

So all you have to do is turn the pages and enjoy!

RBS 6 Nations Round Up

So close and yet so far was the story for England in the 2011 RBS 6 Nations tournament. Looking well placed for a Grand Slam, Triple Crown and a Championship win, Martin Johnson's boys went to Dublin with high hopes. However Ireland had other ideas winning 24-8 to leave England losers on the day but tournament champions.

Weekend One

England's campaign and the tournament as a whole got off to a cracking start in the Millennium Stadium, with their first win there in eight years. Northampton Saints winger Chris Ashton bagged two tries in the competition's first Friday night game. The next day in Rome, Ireland beat Italy by just two points 11-13 and France eased past Scotland 34-21 at home.

Weekend Two

England routed Italy 59-13, with Chris Ashton again the stand-out performer with 4 tries. Fellow winger Mark Cueto also scored a try to break his 18-match drought with Messrs. Haskell, Tindall and Care also touching down. France continued to impress, beating Ireland 22-25 in Dublin, while Wales beat Scotland 6-24 at Murrayfield.

Weekend Three

Returning to HQ, England put the brakes on a French team with eight straight wins under its belt. Toby Flood and Dimitri Yachvilli traded three penalties apiece before Ben Foden scored the only try to set up a 17-9 win. In Rome, Wales beat Italy 16-24 and Ireland squeaked past Scotland 18-21 in Edinburgh.

Weekend Four

A resolute Scotland couldn't quite see off their English visitors, for whom Tom Croft scored the only try. Toby Flood's three penalties proved the difference in a 16-22 win. In the Stadio Flamini, Rome, Italy's 22-21 win was their first ever Six Nations victory over France and was greeted with wild celebrations. In Cardiff Wales beat Ireland 19-13.

Weekend Five

England arrived in Dublin's new Aviva Stadium, focused on the Grand Slam but a Jonathan Sexton-inspired Ireland had other ideas. Brian O'Driscoll became the tournament's all-time highest try scorer, while Sexton kicked 14 points in their 24-8 win. Steve Thompson scored England's try and their muted celebrations showed the difficulty of celebrating winning the tournament while having just lost a match. Runners-up France beat Wales 28-9 and Scotland finally won 21-8 against Italy.

9

The team behind the team

MARTIN JOHNSON
England Team Manager

'Johno' will always be a legend for being the first Englishman to lift the Webb Ellis Cup. After 84 caps his experience is invaluable and while the uncompromising edge on the field may have been exchanged for tough love while coaching the will to win will always be evident.

BEN RYAN
England Sevens Head Coach

England Sevens (and in fact, all age group teams) longest serving coach, Ben Ryan played for England U18, U19 and U21 and led the Cambridge University Sevens team for two years before coaching England Counties. "As a coach", he says "I constantly aim to stretch the players' thinking."

Chris Ashton deserves all the praise he gets for his finishing and Lewis Moody is always ready to put his body on the line but who gets them ready to take on the world? We take a quick look at the coaches behind the England teams.

ROB HUNTER
England Under 20 Head Coach
Rob Hunter was Mark Mapletoft's deputy at the IRB Junior World Championship in Argentina in 2010, then stepped up to the role of head coach in 2010-11. He immediately led his team to a Six Nations Grand Slam and his charges earned huge credit for nearly beating the Baby Blacks in the final of the 2011 JWC.

STUART LANCASTER
England Saxons Head Coach
Stuart Lancaster was the first Leeds player to play a century of games and began playing at the age of ten at St Bees School in Cumbria. He was appointed the RFU's Head of Elite Player Development in 2007 and has held the post of Saxons head coach for the last three years, winning the Churchill Cup in 2010 and 2011.

Lewis MOODY

England captain Lewis Moody MBE has had a long and distinguished career, here we've picked out some of the key moments:

June 12 1978:	Born Lewis Walton Moody in Ascot
Aged 5:	Takes up mini rugby at Bracknell
Aged 12:	Starts playing centre for Oakham School in Rutland
Aged 18:	Studies Business Administration at De Monfort University, Leicester
Aged 18 and 94 days:	Becomes the youngest player to play for Leicester Tigers
Aged18-20:	Understudy to Neil Back at flanker for Leicester Tigers
Aged 19:	Scores two tries for England Colts v Wales
Aged 20:	Wins Madrid Sevens with England Sevens squad
May 19 2001:	Wins Heineken Cup with Leicester Tigers v Stade Francais
June 2 2001:	Makes England debut against Canada
May 25 2002:	Retains Heineken Cup with Leicester v Munster
November 22 2003:	Catches at final line out to set up Jonny Wilkinson's drop goal which won England's first Rugby World Cup
2010 Summer Tour:	Named captain of England and moves to Bath Rugby
2011:	Named captain for Rugby World Cup in New Zealand

SPOT THE DIFFERENCE

Look at the two pictures below, can you spot six differences between them (Mark them on the bottom picture).

THE BIG ENGLAND QUIZ

1. Who did England lose to in the final of the 2011 IRB Junior World Championship in Italy?

2. England head coach Martin Johnson spent most of his career with which famous English club?

3. What is the official capacity of Twickenham stadium?

4. True or false: the governing body for English rugby is called The England Rugby Football Union?

5. Who coached England for two games in between Brian Ashton and Martin Johnson?

6. Which England U20 fly half/centre outplayed his senior colleague Toby Flood to help Saracens win the 2011 Aviva Premiership Final?

7. Which of England's Six Nations rivals is known as the 'Azzuri'?

8. Rory Underwood is currently England's highest try scorer, how many did he score?

9. Can you name the three players playing in the England squad for the 2011 Rugby World Cup playing for French Clubs?

10. Can you name the only two full backs in that squad?

11. Which of England's Six Nations rivals has a dragon as their emblem?

12. Name any of the five uncapped players originally named in England's 2011 Rugby World Cup squad?

13. True or false: England's biggest ever win was 134-0 against Romania?

14. Which club did England legend Jonny Wilkinson play for during the 2010-11 season?

15. Who was England's youngest ever captain?

16. In what year was the first ever game played at Twickenham stadium?

17. Who did England beat in the 2003 Rugby World Cup final?

18. England have won 12 Grand Slams, who has won the next most with 10?

19. For which Premiership club does England winger Chris Ashton play?

20. Which of England's international rivals are known as The Springboks?

Answers on p61

SUPPORTERS CLUB

Juniors

AND GET CLOSER TO YOUR HEROES

SIGN UP FOR ONLY £5

MEMBER BENEFITS INCLUDE

- THE CHANCE TO BE AN ENGLAND MASCOT OR BALL CARRIER - A ONCE IN A LIFETIME OPPORTUNITY
- FREE EMIRATES AIRLINE LONDON SEVENS TICKET*
- SIX EDITIONS OF OUR ONLINE MAG! "GAME ON" PACKED FULL OF COMPETITIONS, INTERVIEWS AND VIDEOS
- FREE ENTRY TO THE WORLD RUGBY MUSEUM AND TWICKENHAM STADIUM TOUR*
- THE CHANCE TO TAKE PART IN A TRAINING DAY AT TWICKENHAM STADIUM

PLUS MUCH MORE

O₂ INVEST IN RUGBY

© 2009 Rugby Football Union.
The RFU Rose is an official trade mark of the
Rugby Football Union and is the subject of
extensive trade mark registration world wide.
*Terms and Conditions Apply

**VISIT RFU.COM/JUNIORSUPPORTERSCLUB
CALL 0871 663 1863**

FROM TINY ACORNS

From tiny acorns mighty oaks do grow, goes the saying. So where did some of the mighty oaks of the England Rugby team start playing?

Courtney Lawes, Lock,
Northampton Old Saints, Currently playing in: RFU Midlands 2 East (South)

David Wilson, Prop,
Westoe RFC, Currently playing in: RFU National League 2 North

Joe Worsley, Flanker,
Welwyn RFC, Currently playing in RFU London North 1

Mark Cueto, Wing
Altrincham Kersal RFC, Currently playing in RFU National League 3 North

Toby Flood, Fly half
Alnwick RFC, Currently playing in RFU Durham/Northumberland 1

Ben Foden, Full back
Chester RUFC, Currently playing in RFU National 3 North

Ben YOUNGS

Leicester Tiger Ben Youngs took to international rugby like a veteran and scored on his first start against Australia in Sydney in 2010. He then scooped the Investec Man of the Match award against the same team at Twickenham in only his second start.

Born in Cawston, Norfolk, Ben was educated at Gresham's School in Holt and first played club rugby for nearby North Walsham. As the son of Nick Youngs, England and Leicester scrum half in the mid-eighties, it was probably inevitable though that he would end up a Tiger.

He joined the Leicester Tigers Academy full time in 2006-7 as a scrum half but at the England Junior National Academy in the same season he was playing at fly half, centre and full back. He became the club's youngest league player in April 2007 when he played against Bristol and came off the bench to finish the 2008 Premiership final against Gloucester.

By the next season he was a key part of the England Under 20s and Sevens squad and was the youngest player at the Junior World Championships in Japan where England lost to New Zealand in the final.

In 2009-10 he won the Land Rover Discovery of the Year title at the Guinness Premiership awards and made his first start for England, scoring against Australia in Sydney after an impressive dummy from a line out.

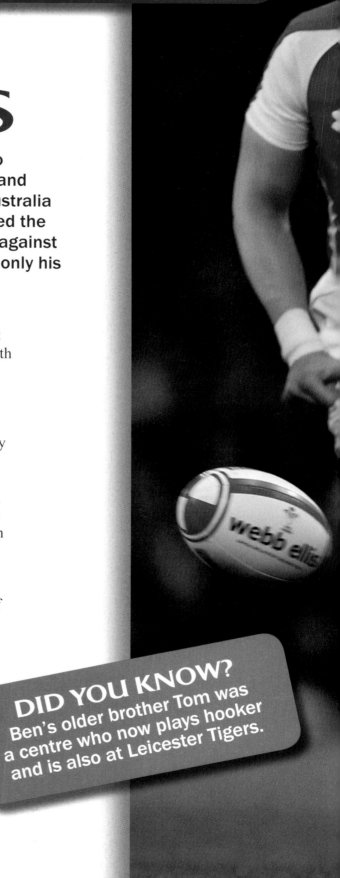

DID YOU KNOW?
Ben's older brother Tom was a centre who now plays hooker and is also at Leicester Tigers.

Elliot DALY

Croydon-born Elliot Daly first played rugby for Beckenham aged five and moved to Dorking RFC in 2009, while there he stepped up from county honours with Surrey to playing for London & SE and then England U16.

He really came to prominence playing for England U20 against Italy in this season's Six Nations, when he scored four tries, following that with a hat trick against Scotland at Newbury.

He has captained the London Wasps A team, is a key member of the academy team and made his senior debut against Leinster at Donnybrook, in a 2010-11 pre-season warm up game. His brother Miles was part of the London Irish academy team and also represented Cambridge in the 2009 U21 Varsity Match.

BIOGRAPHY

Club:	London Wasps
Position:	Centre
Age:	18
Height:	1.84m (6'0")
Weight:	92kg (14st 6lb)

Did you know?

He is one of many accomplished cricketers at Twickenham, having represented both Surrey and England at U15 level.

Joe LAUNCHBURY

Towering lock Joe Launchbury had an outstanding Junior World Championships in Italy in the summer of 2011. His defensive work in England's hard fought win over a very talented South Africa side in particular was highly praised. Not bad for a last minute addition to Rob Hunter's squad at the start of the U20 Six Nations.

Born in Exeter, his first club was Exmouth. He then captained the first XV at Christ's Hospital school in Sussex, where he gained junior county honours. He played in the Harlequins academy between the ages of 15-17 and had a loan spell at Rosslyn Park in National League One.

He scored two tries on his debut for England Under 18s against Japan High Schools at Plymouth. He progressed to be first choice in 2011 for England U20 and was delighted to be part of the team that won the Grand Slam saying "It is the one and only competition that I have won and that includes my schooldays." He also made his Aviva Premiership debut this season against Leicester Tigers at Welford Road.

BIOGRAPHY

Club:	London Wasps
Position:	Lock
Age:	20
Height:	1.98m (6'6")
Weight:	115kg (18st 1lb)

Did you know?

Joe's favourite ground is Roundstone Lane, the humble home of Worthing RFC.

George FORD

The precocious talents of George Ford have already attracted many plaudits, even at the tender age of 18. He was nominated for the IRB's Young Player of The Year award for 2011, despite being the youngest player at the Junior World Championship in Italy, where he was a key part of the England U20 team that gave New Zealand such a shock in the final.

The young Leicester Tigers fly half was also on the shortlist for the 2009 BBC TV Young Sports Personality of the Year award and is currently the youngest player ever to appear in a professional match in England. That match was an LV= Cup game against Leeds Carnegie where at the age of 16 years and 237 days he lined up against his older brother Joe.

He began playing rugby at Saddleworth Rangers rugby league club in Lancashire and also featured for Wigan Warriors and Bradford Bulls before switching codes and joining the Tigers.

BIOGRAPHY

Club:	Leicester Tigers
Position:	Fly half
Age:	18
Height:	1.75m (5'9")
Weight:	80kg (12st 8lb)

Did you know?
George's father Mike is the England defence coach.

Henry THOMAS

Rugby has taken Sale Sharks' powerful prop Henry Thomas all over the UK. He started with Bath minis at the age of six encouraged by his father, who played for London Welsh.

He then went to school at Millfield in Somerset, where he captained the first XV in his last year. He also helped the school win the Rosslyn Park Sevens national tournament twice and eight other sevens competitions in two years. He then moved to Manchester to study Economics at University and signed terms with Sale Sharks, captaining academy side the Jets in 2010-11 season.

A former Number 8, which accounts for his manoeuvrability on the pitch, Thomas has so far represented England at U16, U18 and U19 level. He was also a key figure in the England U20 team which came runners up in the 2011 Junior World Championship in Italy, scoring in the final.

BIOGRAPHY

Club:	Sale Sharks
Position:	Prop
Age:	19
Height:	1.88m (6'2")
Weight:	110kg (17st 4lb)

Did you know?

He is also an accomplished cricketer, representing England at U16 level.

Dan COLE

Coming under the wing of former Leicester Tigers Richard Cockerill and Graham Rowntree helped turn Dan Cole from a good player into a great test player who in 2010 became the first England prop to score a try in 42 matches.

Leicester born and bred he went to Kibworth High School and then Wyggeston & Queen Elizabeth I College and originally played for South Leicester RFC.

He signed for the Tigers in 2006 and after loan spells with Nottingham and Bedford Blues made his debut in a 20-14 defeat by Bath in the EDF Energy Cup.

Dan really began to enhance his reputation when he was a member of the England Under 18 team which won the AER festival in Lille, France. Stepping up the next season to the Under 19s, he played every game of the 2006 U19 RBS 6 Nations and was part of the Under 20s squad for the inaugural Junior World Championship in Wales.

His first big season was 2009 when he started 20 games in the Tigers front row and played all four games for England Saxons. He made his first start for the senior team against Italy in the RBS 6 Nations in 2010 and has racked up 16 caps already.

His finest moment so far came in the game against Ireland at Twickenham when he became the first English prop since Phil Vickery to score a try at the 42nd time of asking.

DID YOU KNOW?
Dan was originally a flanker when he played for South Leicester RFC.

20 Things You Didn't Know About Twickenham

1. Twickenham is sometimes called the 'Cabbage Patch" as that is what it originally was.

2. There is also a local pub called The Cabbage Patch.

3. It's also known as 'Twickers'.

4. It was bought from a man called Billy Williams.

5. It now holds 82,000 spectators.

6. It is the biggest stadium dedicated just to rugby in the world.

7. It originally cost £5,500 to build.

8. It took two years to build...

9. ...and first opened in 1909.

10. England did not feature in the first game.

11. That game was between famous local rivals Richmond RFC and Harlequins.

12. England's first match there was in 1910.

It was against Wales and England won 11-6.

14 It now boasts its own hotel, the London Marriott Hotel, Twickenham.

15 It is also home to the fantastic World Rugby Museum, the finest collection of rugby memorabilia in the world!

16 It has also become known as one of the best open-air music venues in the world...

17 ...The Rolling Stones were the first band to play the stadium in 2000...

18 ...U2, The Police and REM are among the biggest acts to have filled the stadium since.

19 Pre-match picnics in the West Car Park before international matches have become an essential part of the experience.

20 Twickenham hosted the first match of the 2000 Rugby League World Cup.

ENGLAND UNDER 20S AT THE IRB JWC 2011

Pipped at the post!

England U20s at the IRB Junior World Championships in Italy.

After winning the Grand Slam in the U20 Six Nations, head coach Rob Hunter took his side to Italy knowing that they had to maintain their impressive form to win a difficult tournament.

England easily saw off the challenge of home rivals Ireland and Scotland in their first two pool matches but faced a huge match against South Africa to clinch a place in the semi finals. The 'baby Boks' had been scoring tries for fun but Hunter's men matched them. Skipper Alex Gray led his marauding pack to superb effect while fly half George Ford (keeping Aviva Premiership final winner Owen Farrell at 12) marshalled the backs. England scored early in both halves but had to soak up relentless pressure from the 'Boks. Lock Joe Launchbury starred as England weathered the storm to win 26-20.

The semi final in Treviso saw England take on a French side who had booked their place with a classy win over Australia. The first two thirds of the match were very cagey but with wing Christian Wade on fire and George Ford again dictating most of the play England went on to win 33-18.

And so the final and the awesome task of taking on the 'Baby Blacks' in Padua. New Zealand had steam-rolled all their opposition and were keen to put England in their place.

Rob Hunter's men however, were not there to make up the numbers and wing Christian Wade touched down after just two minutes. England went to on to dominate the scrum and put the wind up a clearly shaken All Black pack. Unfortunately the victory wasn't to be, despite matching New Zealand's four tries, the boot of fly half Gareth Anscombe made the difference giving his side a 33-22 win. Hunter's men though came home with their heads held high.

England Counties XV on tour in Spain

England Counties completed their fifth successive unbeaten summer tour when they proved too strong for the Spanish national side in Valladolid. The 'test' win was all the more impressive given that Spain are ranked 23 in the IRB ratings and that the Counties side had an average age of just 22.

As well as beating the national side, England Counties also beat Madrid 53-10 and then Castilla Leon 104-10.

Victory in the final game followed comfortable wins in the two 'warm-up' games against representative teams from Madrid and Castilla Leon. The opening eight-try 53-10 win over Madrid had a reasonably competitive edge, whereas the second match in Salamanca, which the Counties won 104-10, was never a serious contest once the visitors had weathered an early spell of pressure and started to find some real fluency.

"I'm extremely pleased with the way the trip has gone," said Manager Michael Old. "We had three good successes and built on every game, which is the purpose of the trip. We had a good group of lads who came together extremely quickly and stayed together for the whole tour."

"They made our lives extremely easy and were a credit to English rugby and England Counties throughout the trip, thanks in no small part to the great job Gareth Collins did as our tour captain."

Captain Collins said: "The rugby took a little while to get going, but overall I think it has been very successful. It was very enjoyable, the team came together very well and we had a very good end to the tour with the Test match win."

Top Cards

MOST POINTS

Jonny Wilkinson
1,128

TALLEST

Simon Shaw
2.03m

MOST TRIES

Mark Cueto
16

HEAVIEST

Here's a bit of fun with the England Elite squad! You can't buy England Rugby Top Cards but if you could, these would be the best! (All info is pre-Rugby World Cup 2011)

Andrew
Sheridan
123kg

YOUNGEST

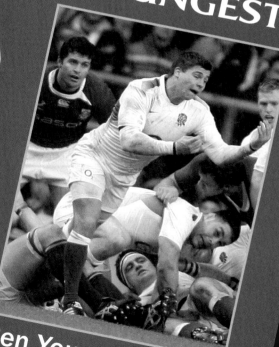

Ben Youngs
21

IN FOCUS

Courtney LAWES

Courtney Lawes made a series of dazzling debuts in senior rugby which have made him, at the age of just 22 one of the best locks in the fiercely competitive test arena.

He was born in Northampton, just a short distance from Franklin's Gardens, the home of the Saints, for whom he now plays as a professional. He went to school at Moulton College and played his first club rugby at Northampton Old Scouts, the club that also launched the careers of Ben Cohen and Steve Thompson.

He played his first senior game in 2007 in an RFU National One league game against Esher but really came to prominence with a man-of-the-match display in a European match against Montpellier while still only a member of the Saints senior academy. He followed that with another dazzling display in his senior debut two weeks later coming off the bench against Harlequins.

He toured Australia with England Under 18s in 2007 but missed the 2008 Under 20 Six Nations through injury but put in some huge performances at both flanker and lock in the 2009 Six Nations and at the IRB Junior World Championship.

He went straight into the England Saxons squad the next season and stepped effortlessly into the Elite squad soon after, following an injury to Nick Easter.

By 2010 he had played in all four of the autumn tests and was named as the Investec Man of the Series.

DID YOU KNOW?
He only took up the game seriously at the age of 16.

SPOT THE BALL

Answers on p61

How good are you at finding hidden words?

```
G P M P D K G T F P E B X
L A X Y R N M P L E T B T
R L L J O R P B R A T E K
E M Y F F Y T T J S W W L
F E R Y Y D N F I Z Y E P
E R Y X D W R L O S H M S
R W K V O W L O G R L W W
E C A R O E C N P O C O M
E G H S M B U K C G O N L
P O R P P O N K V D O N C
E P A H Y S C U E T O A T
H N P T B M S E V E N S L
G Q G R U B B E R M D H F
```

Find and circle all 20 of the England and rugby-related words we've hidden here. Remember, the words could be written vertically, horizontally, diagonally or even backwards.

MOODY	PALMER	FORD	REFEREE	WEBB
YOUNGS	WOOD	ROWNTREE	LOCK	ELLIS
CUETO	HAPE	SEVENS	PROP	GRUBBER
LAWES	CROFT	DROP GOAL	FLAG	WASPS

Answers on p61

39

WELL I NEVER!

Well I never...dance

DAVID STRETTLE
While at Lymm RFC, his first club, David Strettle's flamboyant style and ability to pop up in unusual places on the field, led to his team mates coining the phrase 'disco rugby'!

Well I never...the kiwis

RIKI FLUTEY
Before taking up UK citizenship and playing for England, Riki Flutey had led the famous 'haka' for every single New Zealand age group team!

I bet there are a few things about the England rugby players you didn't know! Here are just a few...

TOM CROFT

Tom Croft says that some of his strength and ability in the line out can be traced back to his days as a member of the West Berkshire Youth Dance Group.

He was a member of the group for four years from the age of 16 studying and performing modern and street dance!

PAUL DORAN-JONES

While in New Zealand as a teenager Paul Doran-Jones featured for Kings Country, the same team England team manager Martin Johnson had played for while down under!

GUESS WHO?

Whether they are preparing or in the heat of a match the England players can get themselves into some pretty unusual positions.
Can you guess who these players are?
Answers on page 61.

ENGLAND SAXONS

CHURCHILL CUP
Winners 2011

ENGLAND TEAM FOR THE FINAL

ENGLAND SAXONS: M Brown (Harlequins); C Sharples (Gloucester Rugby), H Trinder (Gloucester Rugby), B Twelvetrees (Leicester Tigers), M Benjamin (Worcester Warriors); R Clegg (Harlequins), P Hodgson (London Irish); M Mullan (Worcester Warriors), D Paice (London Irish), M Stevens (Saracens), M Botha (Saracens), G Kitchener (Worcester Warriors), J Gaskell (Sale Sharks), T Johnson (Exeter Chiefs), J Crane (Leicester Tigers, captain)

REPLACEMENTS: J Gray (Harlequins) for Paice 70, N Catt (Bath Rugby) for Mullan 70, J Gibson (London Irish) for Kitchener 7, C Fearns (Sale Sharks) for Johnson 70, M Young (Newcastle Falcons) for Hodgson 65, A Goode (Saracens) for Brown 51, T Ojo (London Irish) for Benjamin.

SCORERS: Tries – Benjamin 2, Gaskell, Sharples, Gibson. Conversions – Clegg 3. Penalties – Clegg 2.

England Saxons win the 2011 Churchill Cup

England Saxons won the Churchill Cup in 2011 for the sixth and final time as the USA and Canada will be entering the IRB test arena in 2012 and the tournament will not be needed.

England won the 2011 tournament on home soil beating Canada 37-6 in the final at Sixways, the home of Worcester Warriors.

The Saxons had broken the Churchill Cup points scoring record in their first game, a 13-try 87-8 win over the USA. They had followed that up with a 41-14 thrashing of Tonga that included three penalty tries. At 15th in the IRB rankings however, Canada were a different level to those two sides and provided a much stiffer test for England in the final.

Although England had plenty of possession they struggled early on and after 20 minutes the scoreboard read 3-3, courtesy of a Rory Clegg penalty and an Ander Munro drop goal for Canada.

However England broke the deadlock before half time when Sale Sharks flanker James Gaskell scored a try and then set up Miles Benjamin for another.

Benjamin grabbed another try on his home ground in the second half as did Gloucester wing Charlie Sharples and London Irish flanker Jamie Gibson. Harlequins fly half Clegg contributed 12 points with the boot as Canada tired and England's fitness showed.

Tom WOOD

Stepping into the elite squad last year to replace the injured Tom Croft should have been a daunting task for Tom Wood but his match-winning debut in the cauldron of the Millennium Stadium proved he was equal to the task.

Born in the rugby stronghold of Coventry, Tom went to Woodlands School and first played at the Barker's Butts club where his father Andy had played National League rugby.

After some injury woes and a spell in New Zealand at North Otago he joined the Worcester Academy under the guidance of former Wales coach Mike Ruddock, who said at the time "Tom is an outstanding young forward, he has a very bright future."

He signed for Northampton Saints this season and made an outstanding debut, being named Man of the Match when they beat reigning champions Leicester Tigers 27-19 in the Aviva Premiership.

His England Saxons call came not long after and his call up to the senior team followed the unfortunate injury to Tom Croft. His impressive debut against Wales in Cardiff was followed by equally irresistible performances in the wins over France and Italy at Twickenham.

DID YOU KNOW?
Barker's Butts the old boys team Tom played for also produced England stars Neil Back and Danny Grewcock.

Aviva Premiership 2010-2011

When the England squad aren't training or playing together, they are starring for their clubs, here we take a look back at the key stats for the England players during the 2011 club season.

Attacking flair

England and Saracens wing David Strettle had a great season on the attack, leading both the Opta Stats tables for 'Defenders Beaten' and 'Clean Breaks'. He made 22 of those and beat 45 defenders. His next nearest rival from the England squad was Matt Banahan with 29 defenders beaten.

Unselfish play

England and Leicester Tigers scrum half Ben Youngs also had another great season, setting up the most tries in the Aviva Premiership. He put in team mates for 10 tries, while his scrum half rival Danny Care contributed six assists. Also good at moving the ball was England number 8 Nick Easter, who was third in the Opta Stats table for 'Offloads' with 25.

Accuracy

In the Opta Stats table for passes made however, Danny Care turned the tables on Ben Youngs, coming fifth in the Opta Stats table with 922, while Ben Youngs came in seventh with 801 passes completed.

Defensive mettle

In terms of tackles made during the season, England and London Wasps flanker Joe Worsley put in 180 tackles, though that only put him sixth in the Opta Stats.

Making it count

2009s top scorer Chris Ashton of Northampton Saints, tied with England colleague Topsy Ojo on 10 tries in 2011, which put them joint second behind Leicester Tigers Alesana Tuilagi. Top points scorer in 2011 from the England fold was Charlie Hodgson who racked 165 points and finished sixth in that table.

Bye bye super Ben, Sevens legend!

The England Sevens squad bid farewell last summer to captain and superstar Ben Gollings after 12 years at the top of the international sevens game. His dazzling career included 70 tournaments and three Commonwealth Games.

He scored 220 tries (only Argentina's Santiago Gomez Cora has scored more) in those 12 years since making his debut as a young player of 19.

Even more impressively, Ben stands alone at the top of the HSBC Sevens World Series scoring charts with a huge 2,652 points – more than twice as many as his nearest rival, Fiji legend Waisale Serevi.

He was an integral part of the side that won four consecutive Hong Kong titles, the last in 2006 secured by his final-play try and conversion. He collected a silver medal at the Commonwealth Games in Melbourne and captained England to tournament wins in Wellington and London in 2009.

As England Sevens head coach Ben Ryan said "Ben was there from Day One in 1999 when the World Sevens Series began and, although he had spells with Newcastle and Quins and overseas, he kept on returning because of his love of the sevens game and the game has a lot of affection for him too."

"It is a shame I won't be able to fulfil my ambition of cracking the 3,000 points barrier or becoming all-time top try scorer, but I've been fortunate to enjoy as much as I have," said Gollings.

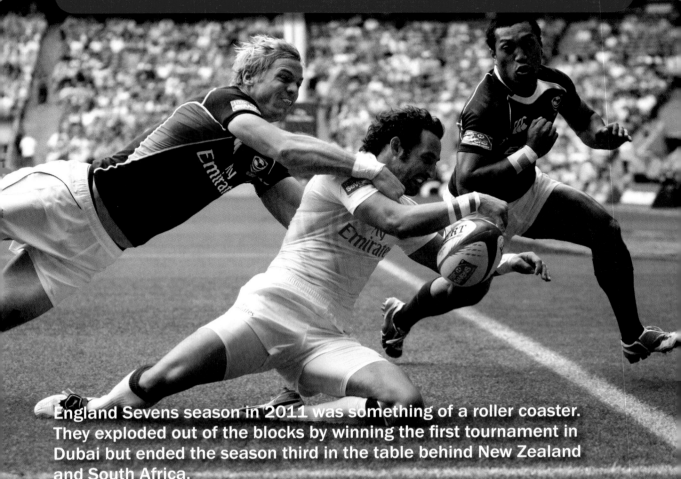

England Sevens season in 2011 was something of a roller coaster. They exploded out of the blocks by winning the first tournament in Dubai but ended the season third in the table behind New Zealand and South Africa.

2011 Round up

The first weekend in Dubai was definitely England's best as they beat New Zealand in the semis and Samoa in the final. It was to be something of a false dawn however, as New Zealand proved to be not just the best team in the series but also England's nemesis.

Unbelievably, the All Blacks beat England in three of the next four finals, in South Africa, New Zealand and in Hong Kong. Furthermore they lost to South Africa in the semi finals amid the bright lights of Las Vegas, USA.

Even though Nick Boyle topped the scoring charts with 8 tries England then lost again to South Africa in the semi finals in Adelaide, Australia.

Back on home soil at the Twickenham Sevens, a poor pool performance was somewhat assuaged by winning the shield. However, the final tournament at Murrayfield, Scotland was the only one of the season not to see England in a semi final.

Predictably, Ben Gollings finished his last season as top scorer with 278 points.

ENGLAND
SE7ENS

ENGLAND SQUAD PROFILES

DELON ARMITAGE

CLUB: London Irish
POSITION: Full back
AGE: 27
HEIGHT: 1.91m
WEIGHT: 94kg
CAPS: 19
POINTS: 34 – 5T, 2PG, 1DG

CHRIS ASHTON

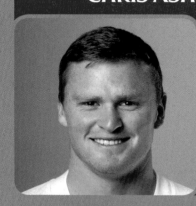

CLUB: Northampton Saints
POSITION: Wing
AGE: 24
HEIGHT: 1.86m
WEIGHT: 92g
CAPS: 12
POINTS: 55 – 9T

MATT BANAHAN

CLUB: Bath Rugby
POSITION: Wing
AGE: 24
HEIGHT: 2.01m
WEIGHT: 112kg
CAPS: 11
POINTS: 20 – 4T

MOURITZ BOTHA

CLUB: Saracens
POSITION: Lock
AGE: 29
HEIGHT: 1.98m
WEIGHT: 113kg
CAPS: 1
POINTS: 0

DANNY CARE

CLUB: Harlequins
POSITION: Scrum half
AGE: 24
HEIGHT: 1.74m
WEIGHT: 85kg
CAPS: 30
POINTS: 18 – 2T, 1DG

GEORGE CHUTER

CLUB: Leicester Tigers
POSITION: Hooker
AGE: 34
HEIGHT: 1.78m
WEIGHT: 100kg
CAPS: 24
POINTS: 5 – 1T

DAN COLE

CLUB: Leicester Tigers
POSITION: Prop
AGE: 24
HEIGHT: 1.9m
WEIGHT: 118kg
CAPS: 16
POINTS: 5 – 1T

ALEX CORBISIERO

CLUB: London Irish
POSITION: Prop
AGE: 22
HEIGHT: 1.86m
WEIGHT: 118kg
CAPS: 5
POINTS: 0

TOM CROFT

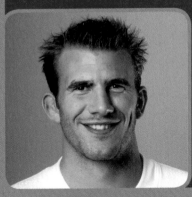

CLUB: Leicester Tigers
POSITION: Flanker
AGE: 25
HEIGHT: 1.98m
WEIGHT: 105kg
CAPS: 24
POINTS: 10 – 2T

MARK CUETO

CLUB: Sale Sharks
POSITION: Wing
AGE: 31
HEIGHT: 1.83m
WEIGHT: 94kg
CAPS: 50
POINTS: 80 – 16T

LOUIS DEACON

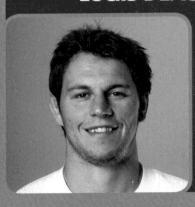

CLUB: Leicester Tigers
POSITION: Lock/ Number 8
AGE: 30
HEIGHT: 1.98m
WEIGHT: 115kg
CAPS: 23
POINTS: 0

PAUL DORAN-JONES

CLUB: Gloucester Rugby
POSITION: Prop
AGE: 26
HEIGHT: 1.85m
WEIGHT: 116kg
CAPS: 3
POINTS: 0

ENGLAND SQUAD PROFILES

NICK EASTER

CLUB: Harlequins
POSITION: Number 8
AGE: 32
HEIGHT: 1.92m
WEIGHT: 114kg
CAPS: 43
POINTS: 25 – 5T

TOBY FLOOD

CLUB: Leicester Tigers
POSITION: Fly half
AGE: 25
HEIGHT: 1.91m
WEIGHT: 93kg
CAPS: 39
POINTS: 193 – 3T, 23C, 43PG, 1DG

RIKI FLUTEY

CLUB: London Wasps
POSITION: Centre
AGE: 31
HEIGHT: 1.83m
WEIGHT: 92kg
CAPS: 13
POINTS: 20 – 4T

BEN FODEN

CLUB: Northampton Saints
POSITION: Full back
AGE: 25
HEIGHT: 1.83m
WEIGHT: 93kg
CAPS: 15
POINTS: 15 – 3T

HENDRE FOURIE

CLUB: Leeds Carnegie
POSITION: Back Row
AGE: 31
HEIGHT: 1.83m
WEIGHT: 108kg
CAPS: 6
POINTS: 0

SHONTAYNE HAPE

CLUB: Bath Rugby
POSITION: Centre
AGE: 31
HEIGHT: 1.87m
WEIGHT: 102kg
CAPS: 11
POINTS: 0

DYLAN HARTLEY

CLUB: Northampton Saints
POSITION: Hooker
AGE: 25
HEIGHT: 1.85m
WEIGHT: 108kg
CAPS: 28
POINTS: 5 – 1T

JAMES HASKELL

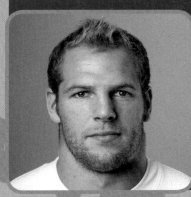

CLUB: Stade Francais
POSITION: Flanker
AGE: 26
HEIGHT: 1.94m
WEIGHT: 111kg
CAPS: 34
POINTS: 15 – 3T

CHARLIE HODGSON

CLUB: Sale Sharks
POSITION: Fly half
AGE: 30
HEIGHT: 1.78m
WEIGHT: 82kg
CAPS: 34
POINTS: 259 – 6T, 44C, 44PG, 3DG

COURTNEY LAWES

CLUB: Northampton Saints
POSITION: Lock/ Flanker
AGE: 22
HEIGHT: 2.01m
WEIGHT: 114kg
CAPS: 8
POINTS: 0

LEE MEARS

CLUB: Bath Rugby
POSITION: Hooker
AGE: 32
HEIGHT: 1.76m
WEIGHT: 98kg
CAPS: 36
POINTS: 5 – 1T

UGO MONYE

CLUB: Harlequins
POSITION: Wing
AGE: 28
HEIGHT: 1.86m
WEIGHT: 92kg
CAPS: 13
POINTS: 5 – 1T

ENGLAND SQUAD PROFILES

LEWIS MOODY

CLUB: Bath Rugby
POSITION: Flanker
AGE: 33
HEIGHT: 1.9m
WEIGHT: 104kg
CAPS: 66
POINTS: 45 – 9T

TOM PALMER

CLUB: Stade Francais
POSITION: Lock
AGE: 32
HEIGHT: 1.98m
WEIGHT: 115kg
CAPS: 25
POINTS: 0

TIM PAYNE

CLUB: London Wasps
POSITION: Prop
AGE: 32
HEIGHT: 1.85m
WEIGHT: 117kg
CAPS: 22
POINTS: 0

CHRIS ROBSHAW

CLUB: Harlequins
POSITION: Back row
AGE: 25
HEIGHT: 1.88m
WEIGHT: 110kg
CAPS: 1
POINTS: 0

CHARLIE SHARPLES

CLUB: Gloucester Rugby
POSITION: Wing
AGE: 21
HEIGHT: 1.83m
WEIGHT: 90kg
CAPS: 1
POINTS: 0

SIMON SHAW

CLUB: London Wasps
POSITION: Lock
AGE: 37
HEIGHT: 2.03m
WEIGHT: 123kg
CAPS: 66
POINTS: 10 – 2T

ANDREW SHERIDAN

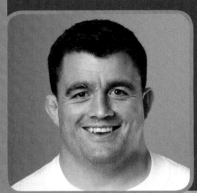

CLUB: Sale Sharks
POSITION: Prop
AGE: 31
HEIGHT: 1.9m
WEIGHT: 123kg
CAPS: 38
POINTS: 0

JOE SIMPSON

CLUB: London
Wasps
POSITION: Scrum
half
AGE: 23
HEIGHT: 1.8m
WEIGHT: 82kg
CAPS: 0
POINTS: 0

JAMES SIMPSON-DANIEL

CLUB: Gloucester
Rugby
POSITION: Wing
AGE: 29
HEIGHT: 1.83m
WEIGHT: 92kg
CAPS: 10
POINTS: 15 – 3T

MATT STEVENS

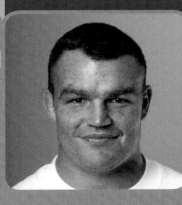

CLUB: Saracens
POSITION: Prop
AGE: 28
HEIGHT: 1.87m
WEIGHT: 122kg
CAPS: 33
POINTS: 0

DAVID STRETTLE

CLUB: Saracens
POSITION: Wing
AGE: 28
HEIGHT: 1.86m
WEIGHT: 87kg
CAPS: 7
POINTS: 5 – 1T

STEVE THOMPSON

CLUB: Leeds
Carnegie
POSITION: Hooker
AGE: 32
HEIGHT: 1.91m
WEIGHT: 115kg
CAPS: 66
POINTS: 20 – 4T

ENGLAND SQUAD PROFILES

MIKE TINDALL

CLUB: Gloucester
Rugby
POSITION: Centre
AGE: 32
HEIGHT: 1.87m
WEIGHT: 102kg
CAPS: 70
POINTS: 74 – 14T,
2C

MANUSAMOA TUILAGI

CLUB: Leicester
Tigers
POSITION: Wing/
Centre
AGE: 20
HEIGHT: 1.85m
WEIGHT: 112kg
CAPS: 1
POINTS: 5 – 1T

THOMAS WALDROM

CLUB: Leicester
Tigers
POSITION:
Number 8
AGE: 28
HEIGHT: 1.85m
WEIGHT: 111kg
CAPS: 0
POINTS: 0

RICHARD WIGGLESWORTH

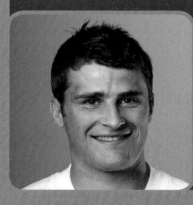

CLUB: Saracens
POSITION: Scrum
half
AGE: 28
HEIGHT: 1.76m
WEIGHT: 84kg
CAPS: 6
POINTS: 5 – 1T

JONNY WILKINSON

CLUB: Toulon
POSITION: Fly half
AGE: 32
HEIGHT: 1.77m
WEIGHT: 88kg
CAPS: 85
POINTS: 1,128 –
6T, 153C, 231PG,
33DG

DAVID WILSON

CLUB: Bath
Rugby
POSITION: Prop
AGE: 26
HEIGHT: 1.85m
WEIGHT: 122kg
CAPS: 17
POINTS: 0

TOM WOOD

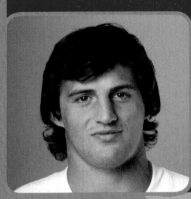

CLUB: Northampton Saints
POSITION: Back row
AGE: 24
HEIGHT: 1.95m
WEIGHT: 105kg
CAPS: 5
POINTS: 0

JOE WORSLEY

CLUB: London Wasps
POSITION: Back row
AGE: 34
HEIGHT: 1.95m
WEIGHT: 110kg
CAPS: 78
POINTS: 50 – 10T

BEN YOUNGS

CLUB: Leicester Tigers
POSITION: Scrum Half
AGE: 21
HEIGHT: 1.83m
WEIGHT: 92kg
CAPS: 12
POINTS: 5 – 1T

QUIZ AND PUZZLE ANSWERS

Wordsearch

G P M P D K G T F P E B X
L A X Y R N M P L E T B T
R L L J O R P B R A T E K
E M Y F F Y T T J S W W L
F E R Y Y D N F I Z Y E P
E R Y X D W R L O S H M S
R W K V O W L O G R L W W
E C A R O E C N P O C O M
E G H S M B U K C G O N L
P O R P P O N K V D O N C
E P A H Y S C U E T O A T
H N P T B M S E V E N S L
G Q G R U B B E R M D H F

Guess Who?
1 Nick Easter
2 Lewis Moody
3 Chris Ashton

England Rugby Quiz Answers
1 New Zealand
2 Leicester Tigers
3 82,000
4 False, it is called the Rugby Football Union
5 Rob Andrew
6 Owen Farrell
7 Italy
8 49 tries
9 Tom Palmer, James Haskell and Jonny Wilkinson
10 Ben Foden and Delon Armitage
11 Wales
12 Mouritiz Botha, Tom Waldron, Joe Simpson, Manu Tuilagi, Charlie Sharples
13 True
14 Toulon
15 Will Carling
16 1909
17 Australia
18 Wales
19 Northampton Saints
20 South Africa

Spot the Difference

Spot the Ball